MAD ABOUT HUMANS

Abhijit Naskar is the twenty-first century mind of science, whose seminal philosophical touch has enabled modern Neuroscience to effectively engage in the human society towards diminishing the ever-growing conflicts among religions. As an untiring advocate of global harmony and peace, he became a beloved best-selling author all over the world with his very first book "The Art of Neuroscience in Everything". With various of his pioneering ventures into the Neuropsychology of religious sentiments, he has hugely contributed in the eradication of religious differences in our world, for which he is popularly hailed as a humanitarian neuroscientist, who takes the human civilization in the path of sweet general harmony.

MAD ABOUT
HUMANS

WORLD MAKER'S ALMANAC

ABHIJIT NASKAR

Also by Abhijit Naskar

The Art of Neuroscience in Everything
Your Own Neuron: A Tour of Your Psychic Brain
The God Parasite: Revelation of Neuroscience
The Spirituality Engine
Love Sutra: The Neuroscientific Manual of Love
Homo: A Brief History of Consciousness
Neurosutra: The Abhijit Naskar Collection
Autobiography of God: Biopsy of A Cognitive Reality
Biopsy of Religions: Neuroanalysis towards Universal
Tolerance
Prescription: Treating India's Soul
What is Mind?
In Search of Divinity: Journey to The Kingdom of Conscience
Love, God & Neurons: Memoir of a scientist who found
himself by getting lost
The Islamophobic Civilization: Voyage of Acceptance
Neurons of Jesus: Mind of A Teacher, Spouse & Thinker
Neurons, Oxygen & Nanak
The Education Decree
Principia Humanitas
The Krishna Cancer
Rowdy Buddha: The First Sapiens
We Are All Black: A Treatise on Racism
The Bengal Tigress: A Treatise on Gender Equality
Either Civilized or Phobic: A Treatise on Homosexuality
Wise Mating: A Treatise on Monogamy
Illusion of Religion: A Treatise on Religious
Fundamentalism
The Film Testament
Human Making is Our Mission: A Treatise on Parenting
I Am The Thread: My Mission
7 Billion Gods: Humans Above All
Lord is My Sheep: Gospel of Human
Morality Absolute
A Push in Perception
Let The Poor Be Your God
Conscience over Nonsense
Saint of The Sapiens
Time to Save Medicine
Fabric of Humanity

Build Bridges not Walls: In the name of Americana
The Constitution of The United Peoples of Earth
Lives to Serve Before I Sleep
When Humans Unite: Making A World Without Borders
All For Acceptance
Monk Meets World
Mission Reality
Citizens of Peace: Beyond The Savagery of Sovereignty
Operation Justice: To Make A Society That Needs No Law
See No Gender
The Gospel of Technology
Every Generation Needs Caretakers: The Gospel of
Patriotism
Aşkanjali: The Sufi Sermon

DEDICATION

Alexandria Ocasio Cortez

CONTENTS

1. Slogan For Humanity
(Sonnet)

Slogan For Humanity (The Sonnet)

Let's slogan for humanity above the
cacophony of politics.
Let's slogan all together for the people
and not bookish morality.
Let's slogan for humanity above the
drumbeats of bigotry.
Let's slogan for the souls in misery and
not nationality.
Let's slogan for humanity above the
foghorn of policies.
Let's slogan cause we are responsible,
not cause we're aggressive.
Let's slogan for humanity above the siren
of world peace.
Let's slogan being peace incarnate beyond
all doctrines illusive.
Let's slogan for humanity above the noise
of traditions.
Let's slogan all together trumping all
worship of sects.
Let's slogan for humanity above the
gunshots of authoritarianism.

Let's slogan as just, free and brave beings,
not loyal subjects.
Awake and Arise my sisters and brothers
to slogan for all of humankind.
We are the light and we are the might that's
needed during this ominous tide.

2. Society Starts With Us

To awake or not to awake - that is the question. Awake from what - you may wonder. Are we asleep - you may ask. Are we not - I ask you. Nay, you ask yourself. When was the last time we opened our eyes – when was the last time we opened our eyes from the never-ending sleep of pride, tradition, heritage, faith, philosophy, intellect, politics and so on? We come out of the mother's womb, then we open our eyes, and soon after that we are put to sleep again - you, me, each one of us.

And those who even dare to open their eyes to really look at the world for the first time, are either forcefully made to fall back asleep or mocked at every step of the way by the rest of the sleeping masses. The sleeping masses hail wakefulness as blasphemy and responsibility as stupidity. While they sleep, they leave all matters of their life to the government - to the political authorities.

And the moment, some of those authorities realize the power that has been placed in their hands by the sleeping society and begin to abuse that power, the masses revolt with utmost aggression, but not due to responsibility mark you, rather because their sleep - their very dear sleep - the comfort of their life, is disrupted. For a while this shouting goes on and after some time like good little obedient children they fall back asleep again, until the next politician comes along to exploit their power.

The point is, people love to shout, *"stop letting criminals into politics"*, while forgetting the fundamental fact that if only they do their part by choosing a representative based on their merit and character, instead of their charisma, no unqualified person can become a politician, no matter how rich, vicious or famous they are. If a criminal becomes a politician, it's the fault of the citizens, not the system, and if a political system keeps failing to oust the criminals from politics, that too is the fault of the citizens.

People love to shout, *"democracy for the people, by the people, of the people"*, yet when it comes to actually practice this principle, their brain turns to dust and their vigor vanishes. It is easier to blame the politicians and civil servants than to take responsibility for the issues of one's own society. Society is us, so its issues are our responsibility - they are the responsibility of each one of us, from the scientist to the civil servant, from the janitor to the teacher, from the preacher to the sex-worker.

No civilized being should be nonchalant about the issues of the society. Being nonchalant is the same as being dead. If you are alive, then that life must, not should, but must act as a crutch to the society. Sign of life is not whether you are breathing, but whether you are helping others. The same goes for a government. A government that helps the citizens is alive, whereas a government that merely presides is dead. A government that puts the growth of a nation at a standstill is as dead as a government that keeps violating plain, ordinary, everyday rights of the humans.

No matter the time and era, if ever a government in any corner of the world, begins to persecute a population on the basis of race, religion, gender or sexual orientation, in the name of national security and prosperity, then it is the existential responsibility of every thinking human to stand up and defy the authority of such heinous, uneducated, megalomaniacal, delusional and self-righteous government.

Remember the Declaration of Justice from *"Operation Justice: To Make A Society That Needs No Law"*.

"In the course of human events, if ever, injustice grabs hold of the landscape that we the people step foot on, it will be our organically divine right to abolish such injustice, with our thoughts, words and actions conscientious. We the people, each one of us, will do our utmost to create a society that needs not the intervention of law or any specialist authority. We will create a society of humans with our own two hands for the humans that are yet to be born, so that they may know justice and order in their life, which we have been deprived of due to the indifference and callousness of our ancestors. We the living, breathing and thinking humans do solemnly declare upon our functional conscience, that from this moment onwards, we will no longer adhere to the traditional habit of dependency, hypocrisy and meekness, and we will come to the aid of every human who faces injustice in any form, with this golden principle engraved upon our hearts, that there are no foreigners, only family."

Only if we are protective of our whole humankind, the way we are protective of our own family, will there be hope for an inclusive and humane society. It's not a matter of political loyalty, it's a matter of human identity. If you are a human, then you must stand up, even if the persecution is being committed by a government you have been loyal to for long. And if you don't stand up, then you have no right to call yourself human. The moment a population becomes complacent towards the actions of its government, that's the moment a nation begins to fall. Rise and fall of a nation are both predicated not on the actions of its government, but those of its citizens.

Therefore, a nation can be truly democratic if the citizens are democratic in their heart – a nation can be conscientious only if the citizens are driven by conscience – a nation can have reason in its veins and not superstitions, only if its citizens practice reason in their everyday life instead of submitting to superstition - a nation can be secular in its true non-hypocritical sense of the term, only if the citizens are secular in their mind.

Secularism can no longer be seen as a mere philosophical word or ideology of the books. Let me give you a simple example. If you are thirsty and you drink a glass of water, is that act of drinking water a philosophy, or is it a plain, ordinary, necessary act of preservation? Likewise, secularism is no more a philosophy, than drinking water is. Secularism is an act of preserving humanity in the humans.

Secularism must be one of the foundation stones of a civilized government – of a civilized nation - of a civilized society. Now here is the interesting part. In practice, secularism is irrelevant in the society of "humans", because a civilized human is naturally secular, whereas a non-secular creature is not a human in the first place, because to be human means having humanity in heart. And there is no place for any kind of segregation whatsoever in humanity.

Humanity means non-sectarianism and this very basic quality of a civilized and thinking human is technically labeled as "secularism". To put it simply, a human society is a secular society, a non-secular society is anything but human. Humanity means non-sectarianism and non-sectarianism is secularism – hence, humanity means secularism.

Therefore, a secular government is a human government, whereas a non-secular government is a government of animals. And whenever in the course of human events segregation begins to creep into the bloodstream of a government, a people must rise empowered by the sense of rights, equality and justice, either to direct such government in the path of humanity or to oust it from power.

Remember, a nation falls not because of governmental atrocity, but because of the citizens' indifference to that atrocity. For once, wake up the human in you and stand up, and even the mightiest government will begin to tremble in front of your conscientious roar. Time and again the need arises for a government to be reminded that its purpose is to serve people, not rule them.

If the people wash their hands of all societal responsibility to act against persecution and oppression, then there is no greater tragedy than that for the progress of a nation. Persecution of a people is not a political matter to be concerned with by the politicians and civil servants only, it's a human matter to be concerned with by all humans.

Segregation is a human matter - injustice is a human matter - discrimination is a human matter - prejudice is a human matter - every single act of inhumanity, no matter who they are committed by, is a human matter. These matters are beyond the petty conflicts born of partisanism. And it is rather imperative that you rise above the primitive party loyalty, in order to see the real roots and nature of the issues that haunt our society. Otherwise, all you will see are the faults of other parties, instead of understanding the real problem.

As long as you are blindly attached to a party, you can never be attached to humanity, and so long as you are not attached to humanity, you can never step up to solve the issues of the problems that trouble humanity. However, let's go very slow here, for these are murky waters, and nothing is black and white. When I say that you must not be blindly attached to any party, it doesn't mean that you cannot work with any political party, rather it simply means, your focus should always be placed on the issues, and not the interest of any party, ideology or any kind of authority.

Let me give you a simple example. Most politicians, nay most humans, have this rigid belief that a person can either be a capitalist or a socialist, but never both. This is one of the most outdated notions held by the so-called modern society. To this day, capitalism is seen by most people as some sort of evil ideology. But the reality is, the problem is not capitalism, the real problem is human greed. Take control of your greed and you would know how to use money for the benefit of all.

3. Beyond Socialism and Capitalism

One cannot walk with just the left foot or just the right foot, one needs both. Even the disabled needs to compensate for the lost leg with a crutch. The very dichotomy between left and right is immaterial while walking, and the same goes for societal growth. So, beware of the intellectual potholes that blind you of plain, ordinary, everyday, practical life.

There are two kinds of intellect, one and the most prevalent is the one that drives you down the road of competition, and the other, rare and pure one is the one driven by curiosity that enables you to walk on the path of investigation. The former leads to argumentation, the latter leads to understanding.

To understand the illusiveness of the dichotomy between left and right, that is, socialism and capitalism, let's place our attention on the fundamental ingredient of this battle - money. Let's investigate the impact of money in the lives of the humans, without taking any side – shall we.

In today's world, money is like oxygen - lack of oxygen can kill you, so can too much of it. Hence, money is neither good nor bad, nevertheless it is an undeniable part of human life. For example, I came into limelight with the publication of my first book. Had that book not been well accepted across the world, I might not have been able to continue with my work, because at that time I was merely a college dropout from a working class family, with no credentials whatsoever.

My first book and several others that followed it, established Naskar as a Scientist and Thinker in front of the world. Eventually invitations for speaking at various institutions began to come in from various parts of the world, which were followed by requests for consultation. Today I am able to carry out my research and writing without worrying about the money, because of the revenue generated in the form of book royalty and speaking and consultation fees.

Now here is the interesting part. The whole world knows me as a humanitarian scientist, because the purpose of my work has always been to unite my humankind, beyond the bounds of race, religion, gender and sexual orientation. But that work of humanitarianism, as people like to call it, is made possible by the monetization of the name Naskar - so in short, it's made possible by capitalism. This may appear a bit repelling to some, but that's the fact of the matter. And that is the fact that drives societal growth. If a nation is not able to monetize its assets, then it'll have to beg for money from the developed parts of the world. Call it capitalism, call it consumerism, call it whatever you like, but the fact remains unchanged.

Growth of a society requires a healthy cooperation between ethics and economy. Ethics without economy leads to physical starvation and economy without ethics leads to mental starvation. It's only with a healthy combination of both can the human society live and progress with health, sanity and serenity.

Ideologies can only get you across a little distance, but once they've served their purpose in a specific time and age, it's imperative that the humans step across those ideologies and walk free into the new era as pioneers of new thoughts, ideas and visions, based on the need of that new time.

In every age the humans must do their own thinking and draw their own maps driven by nothing but a sense of awe and curiosity, while putting aside the old ones. You cannot discover new roads with old maps. So, burn your maps and light up the torch of wonder, curiosity and conscience in your heart – light up that torch and start walking with your head held high and spine upright.

4. Live Torch (Sonnet)

Live Torch (The Sonnet)

Be a live torch amidst the darkest night.
If not you, who else will light up the
society!
Be a living weapon to defend the meek in
fright.
If not you, who else will guard humanity!
Be a breathing sword to scare away
inhumanities.
If not you, who else will draw the
righteous line!
Be a valiant shield to stand against
atrocities.
If not you, who else will call that duty
mine!
Be a daring drum announcing the beats of
acceptance.
If not you, who else will be the emblem of
inclusion!
Be a fierce arrow to penetrate the clouds of
conformity.
If not you, who else will free people from
segregation!

Be the liberating nuke that demolishes all
dogmatic shell.
If not you, who else will burn delivering
the humanizing kernel!

5. Submit To People,
Not Labels

Labels are irrelevant, be it ideological, intellectual, religious, geographical or political. What matters is that you remain free and place your attention on solving the issues, instead of trying to solve the issues exclusively aligned with the interest of any ideology or political party. And in fixing the issues embrace whatever is useful from any and every background. Keep your eyes on the solution and accept whatever works, for such is the way of a thinking human.

The huge brain inside your skull is not there for you to just carry it around, it's there for you to use it. Submit to no ideology, party or figure, submit to people and serve them with all your might, sight and light. And if you find individuals with the sense of responsibility towards the society, then stand by them no matter their political, religious or ideological affiliation. Support individuals, not parties.

So when it's election time, vote the candidate, not the party. Sooner or later all parties get corrupt, but an individual, if truly willing and devoted, can remain uncorrupt, not just throughout the term of service, but all through their life. But this doesn't mean that the individual cannot make mistakes.

We must first learn to distinguish between a mistake and an act of corruption. An action that benefits the self and at the same time harms the society, if committed once, whether out of fear or petty old selfishness, is a mistake, but when such acts become a habit, that's called corruption. Mistakes gotten hold of, are a sign of conscience, whereas mistakes made habit, are a sign of corruption.

Now let's go a bit deeper into the phenomenon of corruption. Humans are born selfish. All biological creatures on planet earth are selfish. Biology without selfishness is nothing but fiction. And, in the modern society of human civilization the apparently stigmatized term "corruption", is born from the biological seeds of selfishness. The so-called corruption is founded upon the brain's innate mechanism of sustaining self-interest. To illustrate this, let's conduct a thought experiment.

Say, a teenage son of an MP hits and kills a commoner on the street with his shining new

Mercedes. Now, what do you think his father would do, when he learns about his son's glorious deed? He would use all his authoritative power to save his son, from being punished by the court system.

Once the father succeeds in saving his son, what do you think the common people of the nation and the media would speak about? They would naturally start having burning discussions about how the politicians abuse their power for serving personal interests.

Now, for the sake of the experiment, let's turn the situation around. Say, a few years later, one of those common people, who was so upset about the disgraceful abuse of power, becomes a politician himself. Now, say he buys his son a beautiful Ferrari, and the son hits a pedestrian just like the last time. Now what do you think this father would do?

He would do the exact same thing that the last politician did. He would do everything in his capacity to save his son. And this is not politics, it's plain ordinary human behavior. In almost all cases, any mentally lucid father or mother would do the same thing. The only possible way to avoid such disastrous circumstances is to give the child a proper healthy upbringing, with a balanced level of love, pampering, and discipline.

Such parental behavior towards the children has nothing to do with politics. It is plain human psychology that has evolved not over a few hundred years, but through millions of years. It is an evolutionary fact that humans care for their offspring more than they care for siblings or non-relatives.

However, it is not an exclusive characteristic of the human race. Rather it is a common behavioral trait seen vividly throughout the animal kingdom, especially in mothers towards the children. They may incubate them, either in nests or in their own bodies, feed them at enormous cost to themselves, and take great risks in protecting them from predators. To take just one particular example, many birds perform a 'distraction display when a predator such as a fox approaches.

A great number of species from many families of birds use a pretense of injury to protect their nests. It is most elaborate in birds that nest in the open on the ground, where the eggs and young are more vulnerable than those of tree-nesting species.

When a predator approaches, the parent bird usually makes no attempt to cover the nest or the young. Instead it limps away from the nest, holding out one wing as though it were broken. The predator sensing easy prey is lured away from the nest containing the chicks. Finally the parent bird gives up its pretense and leaps into the air just in time to escape the fox's jaws. Thus it saves the life of its children in the nest, but at great risk to itself.

Just imagine, if a bird is so evolutionarily protective of its babies, then what can a human do for their children. At any given situation, a person always gives preference to the preservation of his or her own family, over the rest of the society or even the whole nation.

Corruption is simply self-preservation gone astray. It is one thing to commit acts that benefit the self and completely another to do so at the cost of harming others. Self-preservation is not wrong, but when committed at the cost of harming others, is not just wrong, but downright inhuman. That's the characteristic which can be hailed as corruption. And here is an interesting fact of the matter.

When we talk about corruption, people mostly think about powerful politicians or bureaucrats or cops abusing their power, but that's only part of the whole picture, and that too a very small part. Yes you heard right. Corruption of the politicians, bureaucrats, cops and other similar officials is only a small portion of the corruption that haunts a nation.

Think of the infinite acts of irresponsibility committed by everyday ordinary people across the world in daily walks of life, especially in the developing countries. It's only an irresponsible citizenry that makes way for the rise of a corrupt politician. The more irresponsible the citizens, the more corrupt their leaders. It is more important for a nation to have responsible citizens than responsible leaders. If the citizens are responsible, then no politician can dare to abuse their power.

The point is, the humans do not know their own strength. If they did, they wouldn't have needed the voices of MLK, Mandela, Franklin, Bose,

Tolstoy, Seneca, Teresa, Bernie, AOC, Naskar, Chomsky or any other. However, fact of the matter is, we may wish for everyone to become their own voice of reason and their own strength overnight, but it's not going to happen. Because that's not how biology works, that's not how nature works.

Nature has its own pace and its own ways. And when it comes to transforming a society, the ways are rather messy, unpredictable and time consuming. It goes something like this. One person lights up a candle in their heart, and from that one candle a hundred more receive their strength, and then from those hundred, a few thousands. And when a handful of individuals light up their candle across the world, the entire humanity basks in its warmth, grace and glory. It's a process slower than a sloth, but it's absolutely worth it, for the alternative is far too inhuman to even consider.

Now comes the real question. What is the role that you are going to play? Are you going to play the role of the weakling waiting for someone else to light their candle, or are you going to become the light yourself!

This doesn't mean that you have to become a politician or a bureaucrat or a scientist or a philosopher. It simply means that you must awake from your sleep of indifference and rise as a responsible human being. It simply means that you must act responsible in your everyday walk of life, even when everybody else around you is acting irresponsible and mocking you for being responsible. Be a glaring example in the crowd, not another insignificant face in the crowd.

But again, here comes another crucial point to keep in mind. Being a glaring emblem of responsibility in the crowd doesn't mean looking down on the crowd as inferior beings. So, never let your sense of responsibility be taken over by egotistical pride. Do the responsible thing, but as a sentient human, not as yet another self-obsessed, sociopathic egomaniac. Under no circumstances, you should let darkness fester in your mind. Never forget, darkness cannot be eliminated with darkness. Only light can do that.

You can't eliminate the darkness of the society if your own heart is dark itself. So, first you must step beyond darkness. Now the question is, what does it even mean to go beyond darkness! Does it mean that there wouldn't be any darkness in the mind! No, it doesn't mean that, for it is biologically impossible for a human mind to be free from all darkness. So, that's not what going beyond darkness means.

First we must understand what the term darkness refers to. Darkness is simply a metaphorical reference to the inhumanities of the human mind. So, going beyond darkness means, never letting your inhumanities take hold of your psyche - never letting your inhumanities drive your behavior – never letting your inhumanities overpower your humanity. Your behavior must be driven by the civilized part of your mind - by your conscience.

Wake up your conscience and hold it high as a beacon, so that the whole world can bask in its sanctimonious kernel of humaneness. Humaneness won't arrive into our world from some extraterrestrial kingdom, for all the humaneness that the world needs, is already within us. We are the source of humaneness, as well as the vessel of humaneness.

Mark this, if the world stays inhuman, it's because of us and if the world turns human, it's because of us. So, we have a choice to make. You have a choice to make. Are you going to make the world humane or are you going to maintain your silence, while a broken world keeps breaking countless wings of ambition - while it keeps shattering countless dreams of greatness - while it keeps slaughtering countless spirits of glory!

Very few of these atrocities get recognized and punished by the law, but remember, outside the government, beyond the police, there is a law - a law which is impervious to political pressure - a law which is invincible to bureaucratic manipulation - a law which is incorruptible by greed - a law which is uninfluencable by the power of authority. That law is the law of human character.

A being of character never stays silent in the face of inhumanity, regardless of whether the person is a politician, civil servant, scientist, teacher, doctor, construction worker, janitor or anyone else. Character is not defined by the color of your collar, or the color of your skin, it's defined by your gesture when you encounter a complete stranger in trouble, regardless of whether there is a third person to observe your gesture. Real character of a person is revealed when nobody is watching.

Outfits don't define your character, bodily attractiveness doesn't define your character, only your behavior does. Great achievements are born, not from fancy suits, but from great minds. And great minds do not need suits to feel and look important. Only the shallow look at outfits, but the wise knows to look beyond - to look at the person.

Look at the person beyond the outfit my friend. Only then perhaps, just perhaps, we would be able to build a society where humans will give importance to character over everything else - only then we will be able to build a society that's genuine and not fake and shallow. Remember, external appearance fades away in time, but appearance of the mind is timeless – beauty of the mind is timeless.

The conventional notions of beauty and attractiveness are hardwired within our neural circuits and they are meant to steer us in the right direction of survival – survival mark you, not progress or civilized behavior. This means that when you find a person beautiful or attractive, it doesn't mean that the person is a good human being, rather it simply means that the instinctual circuits of your brain is telling you that that person would make a perfect mate for you have babies with.

So, now the point is, such behavior may have served its purpose in the jungle, but in a civilized and conscientious society such behavior is quite out of place. But deeming it out of place doesn't magically wipe it out from our brain's millions of years old circuitry. No matter how much we try we still won't be able to eliminate those instinctual carvings of our neuroanatomy for millions of years, but what we can do is be conscientious enough to not let them drive our behavior.

We must foster the capacity to look at the beauty of a person's mind, before we look at the beauty of a person's body. Only when the individual develops the capacity to look at the beauty of the mind instead of the beauty of the body, can the world develop the capacity to do the same.

Beauty of the world is predicated on our very perception of beauty. If we consider bodily attractiveness as beauty, then the world will always remain shallow, snobbish, fake and inwardly insecure. To change the paradigm of beauty, we must change our very outlook of beauty. Beautiful is not the one with an attractive body, but the one with a kind heart. There is no greater beauty than that of the mind that runs to help those in misery.

Remember, when you are finally lying on your bed for death to knock on your door, it won't matter whatsoever how much money you have earned, the only thing that'll matter is how many people you've helped. If your life improves the lives of even five people, then your life is successful, but if you live even a hundred years earning billions of dollars, without willingly improving the life of even one person, then your entire life is a waste. It's better to not be born than to live such a wasted life. So, do not, I repeat, do not chase after the idea of becoming a billionaire, but chase an idea that not just resonates with your soul, but also holds the potential to lift others.

6. Those Who Call You Mad
(Sonnet)

Those Who Call You Mad (The Sonnet)

Those who call you mad will one day
worship you,
For no great achievement is possible
without madness.
Those who laugh at you will one day learn
from you,
For working through the laugh is a criteria
for greatness.
Those who know not you exist will one day
seek your guidance,
For your endless sacrifice will make you a
beacon.
Those who find you absurd will one day
bow in veneration,
For the absurd ideas take us to the most
breathtaking destination.
Those who look down on you will one day
look up to you,
For your sacrifice will place you on a
pedestal of glory.
Those who are deaf to you will one day
cross limits for you,

For your voice will echo in the hearts as a
purifying symphony.
Those who see you inconsequential will
one day pay you homage.
Breathe your mission, live your mission
and your acts will forge fate's foliage.

7. The Idea is You

The world will not remember the hundred ideas that you talk about now and then, it will remember only the one idea that you practice your whole life as gospel. So, pick up an idea and give your everything to that idea. If you want to sing, then sing with all your might. If you want to paint, paint with all your might. If you want to do math, do math with all your might. If you want to do science, do science with all your might. If you want to serve through politics or civil service, serve with all your might.

Whatever you do, do it with your whole being. Become one with that act. Forget thirst, hunger, sleep, sex, and give your whole existence to one idea - an idea to which you can boldly and unhesitantly point and say *"this idea is me"*. You and your idea must become one, for that idea to become a reality. However, this doesn't mean that you won't have doubts at times, especially during the times of utter darkness. Of course you will have doubts. That's what makes us human. If we don't have doubts, it would only mean that we are not living no more.

Doubts are part of living. However, doubts are not necessarily good or bad. Sometimes doubts can help you mend your errors, and other times they only discourage you. So, you must stay awake to observe the doubts with as little bias as possible. The very evolutionary purpose of a doubt is self-preservation - to keep you from harm's way.

But here the fact is, sometimes you have to put yourself in the harm's way to pave your own path. So, harm or no harm, use your doubts only as a means to mend your errors. To err is human, but to mend the error is even more human. So, stay awake, make mistakes, own your mistakes, correct those mistakes and stop at nothing.

Occasionally even I fall short in the strength department, and in those times of heartache and loneliness, never do I say, *"please, take away my weakness"*, instead I utter, to whom I don't know, and I don't care, *"give me strength"*. Or perhaps, I do know to whom I am saying it, but it took me a long time to accept the hard reality of the matter.

As long as I keep it a secret as to who is the source of my strength, people will speculate and bring in all sorts of mystical notions, due to the lack of facts, but the moment I reveal to you most blatantly and rather clearly that, I am the source of my own strength, then suddenly all the mysticism and mystery vanish into thin air, and what remains is the exuberant radiance of truth.

Nature is truth, so to understand the truth one must understand nature, and that too trumping all personal urges and beliefs. We may never know the absolute reality of nature, but at least, so long as there is breath in our lungs and blood in our veins, we can attempt to wonder, question and discover, otherwise, what is the point of possessing the most magnificent biological organ in the entirety of the known universe!

Never, I repeat, never back down from the truth, even if it goes against your most beloved and comforting beliefs. Remember, more important than the search for truth is acceptance of ignorance. Do you know what you don't know? That's the most crucial question in the search for truth. Understanding of truth begins with the acceptance of ignorance.

Truth has no nature, for truth is nature. Nature does not abide by any superficial man-made law, except for the laws of its own, which we are only beginning to understand. Understand nature and you'll understand truth. And nature includes everything, both the things around us and ourselves.

Now here the question is, is there any such thing as an ultimate truth? The question has bothered philosophers and scientists for ages. But, the reality is, the question itself is an abstraction - a conceptualization of the unknown. It's like giving a name to something which we are yet incapable of knowing. Now, if we are so incapable, why on earth do we need to waste our energy and resources on understanding an imaginary concept which we invented ourselves in the first place to define not our capacity but our inability! The reality may be nothing like it.

So, why don't we simply begin to exercise all your mental faculties to understand the actual truth which is all around us and within us, instead of ceaselessly conceptualizing to boast an imaginary intellectual brilliance! If there is an ultimate truth to the whole universe, we shall eventually get there, when we are mentally mature enough, but we cannot simply make a radical jump to that imaginary futuristic truth. We have to walk on truth as it is now, without distortion, without biases. If one is capable of doing that, then the ultimate truth may simply reveal itself automatically.

So, throw away all your notions of an illustrious ultimate truth, and see with an ordinary nonjudgmental eye. It is only by being ordinary you get to be extraordinary. Being ordinary does not mean being a robotic slave to the social conformities, like everybody else, rather it means not giving importance to both the superficiality, that is the material, and the so-called spiritual.

See the world as it is, at this very moment, without the sociological blinders covering your eyes. Materialism is a blinder, so is the mystical notion of spiritualism. The whole world is basically divided into two parts - one consists of people who think that material riches is everything, and the other consists of people who think spiritual riches is everything.

Both these people suffer from perceptual delusions, driven by their own knacks and urges. The materialists take pleasure in the material, whereas the spiritualists take pleasure in what they think to be spiritual. However, though the materialists are broken up in their perception as well, they are at least not imagining stuff, unlike the spiritualists who think of their imagination to be a supreme truth.

Truth is beyond limitations and beyond imagination. Both the materialists and the spiritualists want to have security in their perceptions of the world. And where the perception is driven by the urge for security, instead of freedom, there can be no truth. And this urge for security is the cause of all sorrow and chaos in the world. And this insecurity intensifies the weakness of us humans to extreme proportions.

But here is the interesting part. Like weakness itself, insecurity as well is born from the mind. So, when faced with difficulty, ask the universe that lies dormant within you, *"let me be brave"*, and all the bravery that you need will burst out through your veins at your rescue.

The power of the universe is in your veins. So, when you are at your wits' end, for once let go of your troubles, and say out loud - *"give me strength"*. It doesn't matter whatsoever to whom you say it. Just say it, because regardless of whether someone is listening to your cry for help, the universe inside your mind is always listening. And when it's made aware of your desperation, it'll rush to your aid and fill you with vigor from inside.

Weakness is a state of mind, so is strength - confusion is a state of mind, so is clarity - zeal is a state of mind, so is insecurity. It all starts in the mind and ends in the mind. One who knows this, beyond mere knowing, like one knows what it feels like to drink a glass of water after spending hours thirsty, never succumbs to weakness, fear and insecurity, instead embraces them as natural part of life.

The best way to step beyond weakness is to embrace it. We are all weak at times, we are all strong at times - we are all confused at times, we are all clear at times - we are all insecure at times, we are all zealous at times. These are what make us human. So, we cannot erase any of them no matter how much we try. What matters is that we make our will towards our mission so strong that our feet never stop walking - let them tremble when they do, but even with your trembling feet and bleeding heart keep walking - keep living - keep living as an insignia of your mission - keep living as the idea that gives meaning to your life.

Make your mission your life - make that one idea your lifeblood - make that one purpose the breath of your existence. Many people have asked me, how would we know about the purpose of our life! The purpose of life is not something that you randomly choose from a stack of ideas - the purpose of your life - the mission of your life - is the one idea that makes you restless - the one idea that doesn't let you sleep at night - the one idea without which you feel like you cannot breathe. And when you imagine your life without that idea, it feels like someone's holding your face under water forcefully, and you are struggling for air. If you have such a yearning, not a fleeting interest mark you, but a yearning, for an idea, then that's your mission.

And if your mission is to break your society free from the confinement of inhumanities, all you gotta do is be annihilated in the service of others. Remember, the only way to lead a people is to serve the people. So, serve with all your might, mind and manners. But mark you, you cannot lift the society while treating it as garbage. And if, for the sake of argument we assume that the society is indeed garbage, then you are a part of that society as well - so what does that make you – I am a part of that society as well - so what does that make me?

The point is, people are stupid at times, but guess what - so are you - so am I. So, let's accept each other's stupidity and fill in for each other's weaknesses - let's stand next to each other and become the strength to each other. I want to be next to every single person on earth, because I know first hand what it is like to have no one by your side.

8. Give Me Blood and Sweat
(Sonnet)

Give Me Blood and Sweat (The Sonnet)

Give me your pleasures, I'll give you
awakening.
Give me your pride, I'll give you inclusion.
Give me your self-obsession, I'll give you
acceptance.
Give me your arrogance, I'll give you
liberation.
Give me your tradition, I'll give you
revolution.
Give me your blindness, I'll give you
clarity.
Give me your disparities, I'll give you
humaneness.
Give me your rigidity, I'll give you
serenity.
Give me your religion, I'll give you
harmony.
Give me your language, I'll give you amity.
Give me your identity, I'll give you unity.
Give me your nationality, I'll give you
humanity.
Give me your sleep and comfort, I'll give

you assimilation.
Give me your blood and sweat, I'll give
you ascension.

9. Serve To Lead

You won't find Christ in the church - you won't find Krishna in the temple - you won't find Jehovah in the synagogue - you won't find Allah in the mosque - the only place they reside is in the humans. Lend a hand to a human in misery and it'll be the highest service to the lord. The whole society is a church and the people are god incarnates, so serve the people, and you'll be serving god - serve the society and you'll be serving god.

Serve to lead, not, lead to serve. And I am mentioning this specifically because I have come across many people who most boastfully shout that they want to become so-called "leaders". I say so-called because that's not how leadership works - genuine leadership - true leadership. You don't become leader by wanting to be a leader, you become a leader by serving people, through whichever field that resonates with you.

In short, you can become a leader only if you have an unquenchable thirst to serve. You can become a leader only if you do not give a damn about being a leader, instead your whole existence reverberates with the joys and sorrows of others. Such is the character of a true leader.

Real leaders, though conceived by the people as leaders, at heart are servants. Hence true leaders are servant leaders. Service is the only path to true greatness. It doesn't matter what your color is - it doesn't matter whether you are a believer or nonbeliever - it doesn't matter whether you are smart - it doesn't matter how well dressed you are - the only measure of greatness is your indefatigable spirit to serve.

And that's the only way we can even dream of building a humane world – that is, with the madness to serve. Otherwise, no matter how much a bunch of intellectuals and celebrities cry "peace, peace", there will never be any peace. Peace begins with sacrifice of selfishness. So long as we are selfish about the exclusive peace and security of our own family and turn a deaf ear to the death-cry of others, we'll have a world that's selfish, snobbish, egotistical and inhuman. For the world to become humane, we must turn humane first.

And as for your ego, instead of trying to eliminate it from your psyche, preserve its emotional force and use it wisely only in situations where it'll benefit others. Here, one may wonder, how can egotism benefit others! And the answer is, egotism is an instinctual force - and if unchecked it can wreak havoc in not just your own life, but that of the people around you. However, if you monitor your ego long enough with awareness, then in time you'll develop the capacity to manifest the emotional reserve of your egotism in whichever form you see fit. For example, once you become aware of yourself, you can utilize the emotional reserve of your egotism to exude strength and conscience while standing up to injustice, inequality and discrimination.

Emotions are neither good or nor bad - they are just forces of nature, they cannot distinguish the right from the wrong themselves, and that's where human conscience comes in. Emotions can do whatever you want them to do. Be aware of your emotions and use them as an aid to your mission, as an aid to your life. Life without emotions is not life, so, do not fall prey to all those mystical nonsense of emotion-free or attachment-free life.

Attachment is our stronghold - it is the glue to the fabric of society. In fact, instead of trying to be less attached, we must be more attached. We must be attached, to not just the members of our own family, but to every single person on earth - to not just the neighbor who lives ten feet away from us, but also the neighbor who lives ten thousand miles away.

Attachment is not the cause of our suffering, our selfishness is. Once you find freedom in giving, attachment will become your strength and not weakness. Attachment is weakness only when you are afraid to lose who or what you are attached to. And to some extent that fear is acceptable, because it is evolutionary, but if that fear gets so debilitating that it takes over your psyche and makes you blind towards life, then it's a sign of utter selfishness.

Mark you, there will always be some fear of losing the people we love, in the back of our head, but never, I repeat, never let that fear cast a shadow on your heart, for once you do, your entire mind will turn dark before you even notice it. And remember, selfless doesn't mean not being concerned with the benefit of the self, rather it means, finding the benefit of the self in the benefit of others, which means you truly, genuinely, actually feel a sense of soulful contentment when your action benefits others. It's utterly selfish, yet it's utterly selfless. And that's the beauty of it. Once you become selfish in selflessness, then all the petty selfishness will vanish from our world.

10. Beyond Selfish and Selfless

The duality between selfishness and selflessness exists only in the presence of separation between the self and others, but the moment you destroy that separation at will and see others as reflections of the self, then the very duality vanishes, for the self becomes all and all become the self. In that state, you are neither selfish nor selfless, you are just you - you are you that is in everyone - you are an image of everyone and everyone is an image of you - you are everyone, everyone is you.

I is not just I, I is also One, which is the very symbol of a united humanity, and that united humanity begins with I - that is, it begins with the individual. A united humanity begins with the individual who sees the whole of humanity in the self, and the self in the whole of humanity. It's a two-way street which begins with the first step that you take in your heart. One first step of yours can set off a cascade of footsteps all across the world, as it did for Christ, as it did for Buddha, as it did for me.

All it takes is one first step - a step beyond personal gain - a step beyond expectation - a step beyond insecurity. Unity of this world hangs on a thin thread, and that's the humanity of the individual human - the humanity in you. As long as there is humanity in you, there is the possibility of humankind to stay together - but the moment that humanity disappears, the world will be torn to pieces.

Some may think, what can the humanity of one individual do! To them I say, all the good things that ever came to this world came from a handful of such individuals, not from the masses. The masses would chase any individual that gives them hope, strength and serenity. They would follow any individual who cares to serve them without expecting anything in return. The world will follow any individual who'd rise against all odds and say out loud *"my life is your crutch."*

Some may come adorned with primitive snobbery and mock your sense of responsibility as mere god complex. Say nothing to them unless extremely necessary and utter only to yourself if needed - *"I am not gonna tell you how great I am, my life is the definition of greatness that I leave for you."*

And remember, although there is no age for service, the greatest sacrifice is to sacrifice one's youth in the service of others, for if a person can dedicate their life at its prime to the upliftment of the society, then such a person can accomplish more in five years than an elderly person can in a hundred years. If I can raise even five such godly beings in each nation, I'll consider my mission accomplished. Some people make cars, some rockets - I make Gods.

Hence, I repeat the motto which I've mentioned a few times in my previous works - be Gods and make Gods. How can you make Gods you ask? Just be the fountain of Godliness yourself and your very existence will cause the birth of a few more Gods in one corner of the world or another. It's not a matter of if, it's only a matter of when.

Sacrifice is infectious - one person's sacrifice makes millions wake up from their sleep of indifference - and in a handful of brave and responsible beings it is bound to spark the urge to sacrifice their own lifeforce for the good of others. That's the law of nature. You are either the cause of evolution in the human universe or you are part of it while somebody else causes it.

Love humanity with every single molecule in your body and the world is bound to turn humane. The world needs love, not borders and philosophies and scriptures - without love we are just good-looking animals. One who knows to love, knows to live. My religion is the best. My nation is the best. My language is the best. What is this? Forget religion - forget nation - forget language - love this whole world as your own family. Because the whole world is your family - nay, the whole world is our family. Love each and love all, for love is the only language known to all humanity. Love above all else, that's the motto for the real human.

But here is the interesting part, this love alters not in the sharp turns of life, if it does, then it never was love. For example, if tough circumstances turn you into a racist or bigot, you never were a human in the first place. Humaneness that bends during murky times is no humaneness. Real humaneness stays awake at all times, in all situations.

In fact, real humaneness doesn't let you sleep, if you know that inhumanity is being committed in your society. Humaneness doesn't let you sleep until you step up to the atrocities in your society. It's a sense of responsibility that cannot be turned off.

Now here comes the phenomenon of guilt. But do not confuse it with responsibility. The psychological apparatus of guilt is far more complicated than it seems. First of all, guilt is your conscience giving you a prick for not acting in the right away when you should have. However, in most cases the guilt may not be justified in the first place - because, the very conscience of the masses is conditioned by the thoughts, opinions, biases and beliefs of their environment. So, the conscience of the masses is not the same as the conscience of the individual. Which means, in most cases, the guilt of the people is conditioned by their society - based on the sense of right and wrong of the society.

In short, most of your fears are not your fears - most of your insecurities are not your insecurities - most of your desires are not your desires - because the very foundation of your psyche has been conditioned by your society, hence your very sense of conscience is not really your sense of conscience, but that of your society, unless you wake up one day at your own free will and actually start living a novel life - a life of your own, driven by your own thoughts, your own opinions, your own desires, and more importantly, your own conscience. Once that original conscience wakes up in you, your bucket of guilt will turn almost empty, because that very conscience won't let you stay silent in the face of wrongdoing.

I mentioned "almost empty" because sometimes you may still fail to act in the best possible manner, for whatever reason, since you are a human. However, guilt from such inability or failure will not be as debilitating as during the times when your guilt is programmed by your society - and it would feel more of an everyday disappointment than guilt - in fact, that failure will only make your conscience stronger so that the next time the need arises for you to act, you can jump into action will all your might.

Life stops not when breathing stops, life stops when action stops. So, never let inaction take over, the day you do, is the day you fall. Or perhaps we've been falling all this time, with occasional bursts of actions from a handful of individuals to lift the world up. So, the real question is, who are you going to be - are you going to be the one among the masses who keep falling, or are you going to be one of those rare few bold and brave individuals whose actions lift everyone up? Even if your feet tremble, even if your arms ache, even if your chest bleeds, stop not till you've lifted the world.

11.Stick to Your Strength

In your attempt to lift the world a lot of tools may appeal to you, but never, I repeat, never ever be distracted from your primary tool in an effort to try new ways. You may occasionally try new means, but always stay focused on your primary means. For example, if you are a writer, always remember that you are a writer, and your primary means of service is written words on pages, not spoken words on videos or audios, because once you give in to the lure of video or audio production, your mind would automatically begin to go astray from your greatest strength, the strength of writing, so in an attempt to try new means, you'd end up losing your most effective means. This doesn't mean that you can't engage in any sort of video or audio production whatsoever, of course you can, but only indirectly.

Your direct focus of attention should always be on your greatest strength - if you are a writer, it should be on writing - if you are a musician or filmmaker, it should be on music or filmmaking - if you are a journalist, it should be on journalism, and so on.

Here is the golden principle of growth, recognize your strength, realize your strength and stick to it till your last breath. You don't need to be good at a lot of things, you just need to be excellent at one thing. Find out that one thing - find out that one strength. This doesn't mean that you cannot slip away sometimes, in fact, you will slip occasionally in an effort to try new things, and it is completely fine, but always remember to come back home - always remember to remember your stronghold. So, now comes the most important question, what is your stronghold - what is your strength - what is your fulcrum for lifting the world?

What's your fulcrum? Is it science - is it technology - is it literature - is it filmmaking or music - is it journalism - is it civil service - is it social work - or is it something else? It doesn't matter what your fulcrum or tool is, what matters is that you and your tool become one. Be one with your tool - be one with your method - be one with your path. The path and the pedestrian must become one, for them to do most good in the world.

12. World in Peril (Sonnet)

World in Peril (The Sonnet)

The world is in peril and security is out of
the window.
If now we don't be humans, what's the
point of us!
Humankind is in turmoil and anxiety is
running amok.
If now we don't be responsible what's the
point of us!
Neighborhoods are wailing in fear and
desperation.
If now we don't lend a hand what's the
point of us!
Communities are struggling in crippling
uncertainty.
If now we don't break narrowness what's
the point of us!
Nations are panting to sustain health and
sanity.
If now we don't rush to rescue what's the
point of us!
Nature is revolting to reclaim her kingdom.
If now we don't make peace with her

what's the point of us!
Now is not the time for theorizing and
criticizing.
Forgetting argumentation we must stand
as one people unbending.

13.Liberationville (Sonnet)

Liberationville (The Sonnet)

When the blood is boiling and conscience is
screaming,
Stop not wishing for a messiah to appear.
When the heart is beating and the mind is
restless,
Sit not praying for the miseries to
disappear.
When the veins are burning and nerves are
revolting,
Stay not cooped up in a cocoon of petty
pleasures.
When the lungs are choking and cells are
aching,
Stay not inanimate out of insecurities and
fears.
When the spine is bending and the head is
drooping,
Stay not silent submitting to tribal identity.
When the knees are trembling and the
throat is thirsty,
Stand not frail as servant of conformity.
When the eyes are teary and lips are

dreary, never consider sitting still.
Obliterate loyalty to atrocities of the norm
waking up to liberationville.

14. You Are The Almanac

What is the path - it is a reflection of the pedestrian - what is the pedestrian – they are a reflection of the path - it's all one. And only in this oneness can the best of creation manifest. If you are not one with your path, you are divided, and if you are divided, your creation will also be divided. Division begets division - separation begets separation - be it separation from one's path or separation from one's world.

So, to raise a united world, we the individuals must stand one, with no concern for race, religion, gender or sexual orientation. To put it simply - there should be one sole concern in everyone's mind - I the individual am standing one undivided. Stand as one and the world will unite around you. The very term individual means one without duality - so now the question is, are we really without duality? We are anything but that. Even I am not free from dualities, as you would've realized by now from a few of my statements earlier.

Now let's break down the term duality. What does it mean? Duality means conflict - in this case, internal conflicts of the mind. So, now the question is, is it possible to be absolute free from conflicts? And the simple answer is, no. The biological fact is, it is impossible to have no conflict in your mind as long as you live. So, anybody who says they don't have any conflict, is either lying or deluding themselves.

A mind that has no conflict, is not alive. Conflicts make us alert - conflicts make us awake - conflicts make us observant, which won't be possible in complacency. So, the focus should not be freedom from conflicts, but awareness of conflicts. Therefore the question is not, do you have conflicts? The real question is, are you aware of your conflicts?

Because only if you are aware of your conflicts, that very awareness will enable you to step beyond those conflicts every time they arise in your daily walks of life. And when the individual is capable of stepping beyond their internal conflicts, the world will slowly but surely begin to step across its societal conflicts. There will still be conflicts mark you, but they'd be far less incapacitating.

To end the conflicts of the world, the self must have the capacity in its veins to be aware of its own conflicts, breaking free from the confinement of pride and self-righteousness. Still, we will not be able to end all conflicts of the world, but we can make them powerless, once we rise from the ashes of our self-imposed meekness and destitute.

We are not meek, nor are we destructible - we are meek and frail so long as we think of ourselves as meek and frail - so, break that meekness - break the delusion that you need a messiah to be rescued by from your misery. All the answers to your prayers lie within you, yet you look for them here and there. Look no more my friend and open your eyes - open the eyes of observation - open the eyes of wakefulness and you will not only find the answers that you seek, but the answers to the problems of this world, for in the very depth of your heart lies the almanac of world building. You are the world builder as well as the almanac of world building.

BIBLIOGRAPHY

Aristotle. Politics. Penguin; Revised, Reprint edition. (2000)

Aristotle. De Anima (On the Soul). Penguin Random House. 1987

Aristotle. Physics. Kessinger Publishing, 2004

Archer M., (2000), Being Human: The Problem of Agency. Cambridge University Press.

Archer M., (2003), Structure, Agency and the Internal Conversation. Cambridge University Press.

Adolphs R (2003) Cognitive neuroscience of human social behaviour. Nature Rev Neurosci 4: 165–178.

Adolphs R, Tranel D, Damasio AR (2003) Dissociable neural systems for recognizing emotions. Brain Cogn 52: 61–69.

Afton, A. D. (1985). Forced copulation as a reproductive strategy of male lesser scaup: A field test of some predictions. - Behaviour 92, p. 146-167.

Allison T, Puce A, McCarthy G. (2000) Social perception from visual cues: role of the STS region. Trends Cogn Sci 4: 267–278.

Andresen, Jensine, and Robert Forman, eds. Cognitive Models and Spiritual Maps. Bowling Green, Ohio: Imprint Academic, 2000.

Ashbrook, James, and Carol Albright. The Humanizing Brain: Where Religion and Neuroscience Meet. Cleveland, OH: Pilgrim Press, 1997.

Azari, Nina, Janpeter Nickel, Gilbert Wunderlich, Michael Niedeggen, Harald Hefter, Lutz Tellmann, Hans Herzog, Petra Stoerig, Dieter Birnbacher, and Rudiger Seitz. "Neural Correlates of Religious Experience."

European Journal of Neuroscience 13, no. 8 (2001)

Agar, N. (2004). Liberal eugenics: In defence of human enhancement. London: Blackwell Publishing.

Alteheld, N., Roessler, G., Vobig, M., & Walter, R. (2004). The retina implant new approach to a visual prosthesis. Biomedizinische Technik, 49(4), 99–103.

Antal, A., Nitsche, M. A., Kincses, T. Z., Kruse, W., Hoffmann, K. P., & Paulus, W. (2004a). Facilitation of visuo-motor learning by transcranial direct current stimulation of the motor and extrastriate visual areas in humans. European Journal of Neuroscience, 19(10), 2888–2892.

Bhat Z, Kumar, S, Bhat H (2015) In vitro meat production. Challenges and benefits over conventional meat production. J Sci Food Agric 14: 241–248

Bernstein R. J., (1967), John Dewey. New York: Washington Square Press.

Bernstein R.J., (1971), Praxis and Action: Contemporary Philosophies of Human Activity. Philadelphia: University of Pennsylvania Press.

Bernstein R.J., (1976), The Restructuring Social and Political Thought.

Bernstein R.J., (1983), Beyond Relativism and Objectivism: Science, Hermeneutics, and Praxis. Philadelphia: University of Pennsylvania Press.

Bernstein R.J., (1986), Philosophical Profiles. Philadelphia: University of Pennsylvania Press.

Bernstein R.J., (1991), New Constellation. Cambridge: MIT Press.

Barash, D. P. (1977). Sociobiology of rape in mallards (Anas platyrhynchos):

Responses of the mated male. - Science 197, p. 788-789.

Berger, J. (1986). Wild horses of the great basin: Social competition and population size. - The University of Chicago Press, Chicago.

Birkhead, T. R., Johnson, S. D. & Nettleship, D. N. (1985). Extra-pair matings and mate guarding in the common murre Uria aalge. - Anim. Behav. 33, p. 608-619.

Beauregard, Mario, and Vincent Paquette. "Neural Correlates of a Mystical Experience in Carmelite Nuns." Neuroscience Letters 405, no. 3 (2006)

Benson, Herbert. Timeless Healing: The Power and Biology of Belief. New York: Scribner, 1996

Bogen, J.E.(1995a), 'On the neurophysiology of consciousness: Part I. An overview', Consciousness and Cognition, 4.

Bogen, J.E. (1995b), 'On the neurophysiology of consciousness: Part II. Constraining the semantic problem', Consciousness and Cognition, 4.

Bremner, J. D., R. Soufer, et al. (2001). "Gender differences in cognitive and neural correlates of remembrance of emotional words." Psychopharmacol Bull 35 (3).

Brothers, L. (2002). The social brain: A project for integrating primate behavior and neurophysiology in a new domain. In J. T. Cacioppo et al. (Eds.), Foundations in neuroscience. Cambridge, MA: MIT Press.

Buss, D. D. (2003). Evolutionary Psychology: The New Science of Mind, 2nd ed. New York: Allyn & Bacon.

Buss, D. M. (1989). "Conflict between the sexes: Strategic interference and the evocation of anger and upset." J Pers Soc Psychol 56 (5).

Buss, D. M. (1995). "Psychological sex differences. Origins through sexual selection." Am Psychol 50 (3).

Buss, D. M. (2002). "Review: Human Mate Guarding." Neuro Endocrinol Lett 23 (Suppl 4).

Buss, D. M., and D. P. Schmitt (1993). "Sexual strategies theory: An evolutionary perspective on human mating." Psychol Rev 100 (2).

Blakemore SJ, Decety J (2001) From the perception of action to the understanding of intention. Nature Rev Neurosci 2: 561.

Bruce C, Desimone R, Gross CG (1981) Visual properties of neurons in a polysensory area in superior temporal sulcus of the macaque. J Neurophysiol 46: 369–384.

Buccino G, Vogt S, Ritzl A, Fink GR, Zilles K, Freund HJ, Rizzolatti G (2004) Neural circuits underlying imitation of hand actions: an event related fMRI study. Neuron 42: 323–34.

Colapietro V., (1988), "Human Agency: The Habits of Our Being." Southern Journal of Philosophy, XXVI, 2, pp. 153-68.

Colapietro V., (1992), "Purpose, Power, and Agency." The Monist, 75, 4 (October) pp. 423-44.

Colapietro V., (2003), "Signs and their vicissitudes: Meanings in excess of consciousness and functionality." Logica, Dialogica, Ideologica, a cure di Susan Petrilli e Patrizia Calefato (Milano: Mimesis), pp. 221-36.

Colapietro V., (2004a), "C. S. Peirce's Reclamation of Teleology." Nature in American Philosophy, ed. Jean De Groot (Washington, D.C.: Catholic University Press of America), pp. 88-108.

Colapietro V., (2004b), "Portrait of a Historicist: An Alternative Reading of

Peircean Semiotic." Semiotiche, 2/04 [maggio 2004], pp. 49-68.

Colapietro V., (2006), "Engaged Pluralism: Between Alterity and Sociality." The Pragmatic Century: Conversations with Richard J. Bernstein (Albany, NY: SUNY Press), pp. 39-68.

Colapietro V., (2009), "Habit, Competence, and Purpose." Forthcoming in The Transactions of the Charles S. Peirce Society. Calder AJ, Keane J, Manes F, Antoun N, Young AW (2000) Impaired recognition and experience of disgust following brain injury. Nature Neurosci 3: 1077–1078.

Carey DP, Perrett DI, Oram MW (1997) Recognizing, understanding and reproducing actions. In: Jeannerod M, Grafman J (eds) Handbook of neuropsychology. Vol. 11: Action and cognition. Elsevier, Amsterdam.

Carr L, Iacoboni M, Dubeau MC, Mazziotta JC, Lenzi GL (2003) Neural mechanisms of empathy in humans: a relay from neural systems for imitation to limbic areas. Proc Natl Acad Sci USA 100: 5497–5502.

Changeux JP, Ricoeur P (1998) La nature et la règle. Odile Jacob, Paris.

Cochin S, Barthelemy C, Roux S, Martineau J (1999) Observation and execution of movement: similarities demonstrated by quantified electroencephalograpy. Eur J Neurosci 11: 1839– 1842.

Chomsky Noam, (2017) Requiem for the American Dream

Chomsky Noam, (2016) Who Rules the World?

Chomsky Noam, (2010) How the World Works

Churchland, P.S. (1986), Neurophilosophy (Cambridge, MA: The MIT Press).

Churchland, P.S. & Ramachandran, V.S. (1993), 'Filling in: Why Dennett is wrong', in Dennett and His Critics: Demystifying Mind, ed. B. Dahlbom (Oxford: Blackwell Scientific Press).

Churchland, P.S., Ramachandran, V.S. & Sejnowski, T.J. (1994), 'A critique of pure vision', in Large- scale Neuronal Theories of the Brain, ed. C. Koch & J.L. Davis (Cambridge, MA: The MIT Press).

Crick, F. (1994), The Astonishing Hypothesis: The Scientific Search for the Soul (New York: Simon and Schuster).

Crick, F. (1996), 'Visual perception: rivalry and consciousness', Nature, 379.

Crick, F. & Koch, C. (1992), 'The problem of consciousness', Scientific American, 267.

Craig AD (2002) How do you feel? Interoception: the sense of the physiological condition of the body. Nature Rev Neurosci 3: 655–666.

Damasio, A (2003a) Looking for Spinoza. Harcourt Inc. Damasio A (2003b) Feeling of emotion and the self. Ann NY Acad Sci 1001: 253–261.

d'Aquili, Eugene. "Senses of Reality in Science and Religion." Zygon 17, no 4 (1982)

d'Aquili, Eugene. "The Biopsychological Determinants of Religious Ritual Behavior." Zygon 10, no. 1 (1975)

d'Aquili, Eugene. "The Myth-Ritual Complex: A Biogenetic Structural Analysis." Zygon 18, no. 3 (1983) d'Aquili, Eugene, and Andrew Newberg. The Mystical Mind: Probing the Biology of Religious Experience. Minneapolis: Fortress Press, 1999.

Daly DD. 1958. Ictal affect. Am J Psychiatry.

Damasio, A. (1994) Descartes' Error: Emotion, Reason and the Human Brain. New York, Putnams.

Damasio, A. (1999) The Feeling of What Happens: Body, Emotion and the Making of Consciousness. London, Heinemann.

Darwin, C. (1859) On the Origin of Species by Means of Natural Selection. London, Murray.

Darwin, C. (1871) The Descent of Man and Selection in Relation to Sex. London, John Murray.

Darwin, C. (1872) The Expression of the Emotions in Man and Animals. London, John Murray; also published

1965, Chicago, University of Chicago Press.

Dawkins, M.S. (1987) Minding and mattering. In C. Blakemore and S. Greenfield (eds) Mindwaves. Oxford, Blackwell, 151-60.

Dawkins, R. (1976) The Selfish Gene. Oxford, Oxford University Press; a new edition, with additional material, was published in 1989.

Dawkins, R. (1986) The Blind Watchmaker. London, Longman.

Di Pellegrino G, Fadiga L, Fogassi L, Gallese V, Rizzolatti G (1992) Understanding motor events: A neurophysiological study. Exp Brain Res 91: 176–80.

Deikman, A.J. (2000) A functional approach to mysticism. Journal of Consciousness Studies 7(11-12), 75-91.

Delmonte, M.M. (1987) Personality and meditation. In M. West (ed.) The

Psychology of Meditation. Oxford, Clarendon Press, 118-32.

Dennett, D.C. (1987) The Intentional Stance. Cambridge, MA, MIT Press.

Dennett, D.C. (1988) Quining qualia. In A.J. Marcel and E. Bisiach (eds) Consciousness in Contemporary Science. Oxford, Oxford University Press, 42-77.

Dennett, D.C. (1991) Consciousness Explained. Boston, MA, and London, Little, Brown and Co.

Dennett, D.C. (1995a) Darwin's Dangerous Idea. London, Penguin.

Dennett, D.C. (1995b) The unimagined preposterousness of zombies. Journal of Consciousness Studies 2(1), 322-6.

Dennett, D.C. (1995c) Cog: steps towards consciousness in robots. In T. Metzinger (ed.) Conscious Experience. Thorverton, Devon, Imprint Academic, 471-87.

Dennett, D.C. (1995d) The path not taken. Behavioral and Brain Sciences 18, 252-3; commentary on N. Block, On a confusion about a function of consciousness. Behavioral and Brain Sciences 18, 227.

Dennett, D.C. (1996a) Facing backwards on the problem of consciousness. Journal of Consciousness Studies 3(1), 4-6.

Dennett, D.C. (1996b) Kinds of Minds: Towards an Understanding of Consciousness. London, Weidenfeld & Nicolson.

Dennett, D.C. (1997) An exchange with Daniel Dennett. In J. Searle (ed.) The Mystery of Consciousness. New York, New York Review of Books, 115-19.

Dennett, D.C. (1998) The myth of double transduction. In S.R. Hameroff, A.W. Kaszniak and A. C. Scott (eds) Toward a Science of Consciousness: The Second Tucson Discussions and

Debates. Cambridge, MA, MIT Press, 97-107.

Dennett, D.C. (1998b) Brainchildren: Essays on Designing Minds. Cambridge, MA, MIT Press.

Dennett, D.C. (2001) The fantasy of first person science. Debate with D. Chalmers, Northwestern University, Evanston, IL, February 2001.

Dennett, D.C. (2003) Freedom Evolves. New York, Penguin.

Dennett, D.C. and Kinsbourne, M. (1992) Time and the observer: the where and when of consciousness in the brain. Behavioral and Brain Sciences 15, 183-247, including commentaries and authors' responses.

Dewey J., (1911 [1977]), "Epistemological Realism: The Alleged Ubiquity of the Knowledge Relation." Journal of Philosophy, VIII, 20 (September 28, 1911).

Dewhurst, Kenneth, and A. W. Beard. "Sudden Religious Conversions in Temporal Lobe Epilepsy." British Journal of Psychiatry 117 (1970)

Dewhurst K, Beard AW. Sudden religious conversions in temporal lobe epilepsy. 1970 Epilepsy Behav 2003

Devinsky O, Lai G. Spirituality and religion in epilepsy. Epilepsy Behav 2008.

Devinsky, O., Morrell, MJ, Vogt, BA. (1995) 'Contribution of anterior cingulate cortex to behavior', Brain, 118.

Douglas Stone A., Chapter 24, The Indian Comet, in the book Einstein and the Quantum, Princeton University Press, Princeton, New Jersey, 2013.

E. Horvitz, "One Hundred Year Study on Artificial Intelligence: Reflections and Framing," ed: Stanford University, 2014.

Einstein A. (1925). "Quantentheorie des einatomigen idealen Gases". Sitzungsberichte der Preussischen Akademie der Wissenschaften.

Eckhart Meister, Selected Writings

Egidi R., ed. (1999), "Von Wright and 'Dante's Dream': Stages in a Philosophical Pilgrim's Progress", in In Search of a New Humanism: the Philosophy of G.H. von Wright, ed. by R. Egidi, Kluwer, Dordrecht.

Fadiga L, Fogassi L, Pavesi G, Rizzolatti G (1995) Motor facilitation during action observation: a magnetic stimulation study. J Neurophysiol 73: 2608–2611.

Fogassi L, Gallese V, Fadiga L, Rizzolatti G (1998) Neurons responding to the sight of goal directed hand/arm actions in the parietal area PF (7b) of the macaque monkey. Soc Neurosci Abs 24:257.5.

Frith U, Frith CD (2003) Development and neurophysiology of mentalizing. Philos Trans R Soc Lond B Biol Sci 358: 459.

Farah, M.J. (1989), 'The neural basis of mental imagery', Trends in Neurosciences, 10.

Finlay BL, Darlington RB (1995) Linked regularities in the development and evolution of mammalian brains. Science 268.

Freud, S. "The Interpretation of Dreams", 1900

Freud, S. "Selected papers on hysteria and other psychoneuroses" Journal of Nervous and Mental Disease 1909.

Freud, S. "The Origin and Development of Psychoanalysis", 1910

Freud, S. "Psychopathology of everyday life", 1914

Freud, S. "Beyond the Pleasure Principle", 1920

Frith, C.D. & Dolan, R.J. (1997), 'Abnormal beliefs: Delusions and memory', Paper presented at the May, 1997, Harvard Conference on Memory and Belief.

Gay, Volney, ed. Neuroscience and Religion. Plymouth, UK: Lexington Books, 2009.

Gazzaniga, M. S. (1985). The social brain. New York: Basic Books.

Gazzaniga, M.S. (1993), 'Brain mechanisms and conscious experience', Ciba Foundation Symposium, 174.

Geschwind N. "Behavioural changes in temporal lobe epilepsy". Psychol Med. 1979.

Gellhorn, E., Kiely, W.F. "Mystical states of consciousness: neurophysiological and clinical aspects." J Nerv Ment Dis. 1972;154:399-405.

Gilbert SL, Dobyns WB, Lahn BT (2005) Genetic links between brain development and brain evolution. Nat Rev Genet 6.

Gray JA. The Psychology of Fear and Stress. 2nd ed. New York, NY: Cambridge University Press; 1988.

Gloor, P. (1992), 'Amygdala and temporal lobe epilepsy', in The Amygdala: Neurobiological Aspects of Emotion, Memory and Mental Dysfunction, ed J.P. Aggleton (New York: Wiley-Liss).

Greenspan, S. I. and S. G. Shanker (2004). The first idea: How symbols, language, and intelligence evolved from our early primate ancestors to modern humans. Cambridge, MA: Da Capo Press.

Grady, D. (1993), 'The vision thing: Mainly in the brain', Discover, June.

Gallagher HL, Frith CD (2003) Functional imaging of 'theory of mind'. Trends Cogn Sci 7: 77.

Gallese V, Fogassi L, Fadiga L, Rizzolatti G (2002) Action representation and the inferior parietal lobule. In: Prinz W, Hommel B (eds) Attention & Performance XIX. Common mechanisms in perception and action. Oxford University Press, Oxford.

Gallese V, Keysers C, Rizzolatti G (2004) A unifying view of the basis of social cognition. Trends Cogn Sci 8: 396–403.

Gangitano M, Mottaghy FM, Pascual-Leone A (2001) Phase specific modulation of cortical motor output during movement observation. NeuroReport 12: 1489–1492.

Gangitano M, Mottaghy FM, Pascual-Leone A (2004) Modulation of premotor mirror neuron activity during observation of unpredictable grasping movements. Eur J Neurosci 20: 2193– 2202.

Goldman AI, Sripada CS (2004) Simulationist models of face-based emotion recognition. Cognition 94: 193–213.

Grèzes J, Costes N, Decety J (1998) Top-down effect of strategy on the perception of human biological motion: a PET investigation. Cogn Neuropsychol 15: 553–582.

Grèzes J, Armony JL, Rowe J, Passingham RE (2003) Activations related to "mirror" and "canonical" neurones in the human brain: an fMRI study. Neuroimage 18: 928–937.

Gross CG, Rocha-Miranda CE, Bender DB (1972) Visual properties of neurons in the inferotemporal cortex of the macaque. J Neurophysiol 35: 96–111.

Hari R, Forss N, Avikainen S, Kirveskari S, Salenius S, Rizzolatti G

(1998) Activation of human primary motor cortex during action observation: a neuromagnetic study. Proc. Natl Acad Sci USA 95: 15061–15065.

Hardy, G. H. (1940). Ramanujan. Cambridge: Cambridge University Press.

Hall, Daniel, Keith Meador, and Harold Koenig. "Measuring Religiousness in Health Research: Review and Critique." Journal of Religion and Health 47, no. 2 (2008)

Harris, Sam, Jonas Kaplan, Ashley Curiel, Susan Bookheimer, Marco Iacoboni, and Mark Cohen. "The Neural Correlates of Religious and Nonreligious Belief." PLoS One 4, no. 10 (October 1, 2009)

Halgren, E. (1992), 'Emotional neurophysiology of the amygdala within the context of human cognition', in The Amygdala:

Neurobiological Aspects of Emotion, Memory and Mental Dysfunction, ed J.P. Aggleton (New York: Wiley-Liss).

Halligan PW, Fink GR, Marshal JC, Vallar G. 2003. Spatial cognition: evidence from visual neglect. Trends Cogn Sci.

Handbook of Emotions, Edited by Michael Lewis, Jeannette M. Haviland-Jones, and Lisa Feldman Barrett, The Guilford Press; 3rd edition (2010).

Haggard, P., Clark, S. and Kalogeras,]. (2002) Voluntary action and conscious awareness, Nature Neuroscience 5, 382-5. Haggard, P., Newman, C. and Magno, E. (1999) On the perceived time of voluntary actions. British Journal of Psychology 90, 291-303.

Hameroff, S.R. and Penrose, R. (1996) Conscious events as orchestrated space-time selections. Journal of Consciousness Studies 3(1), 36-53; also reprinted in J. Shear (ed.) (1997)

Explaining Consciousness-The Hard Problem. Cambridge, MA, MIT Press, 177-95.

Hardcastle, V.G. (2000) How to understand theN in NCC. InT. Metzinger (ed.) Neural Correlates of Consciousness. Cambridge, MA, MIT Press, 259-64.

Harding, D.E. (1961) On Having no Head: Zen and the Re-Discovery of the Obvious. London, Buddhist Society.

Hardy, A. (1979) The Spiritual Nature of Man: A Study of Contemporary Religious Experience. Oxford, Clarendon Press.

Hamad, S. (1990) The symbol grounding problem. Physica D 42, 335-46.

Hamad, S. (2001) No easy way out. The Sciences 41(2), 36-42.

Harre, R. and Gillett, G. (1994) The Discursive Mind. Thousand Oaks, CA, Sage.

Haugeland, J. (ed.) (1997) Mind Design II: Philosophy, Psychology, Artificial Intelligence. Cambridge, MA, MIT Press.

Hauser, M.D. (2000) Wild Minds: What Animals Really Think. New York, Henry Holt and Co.; London, Penguin.

Hearne, K. (1990) The Dream Machine. Northants, Aquarian.

Hebb, D.O. (1949) The Organization of Behavior. New York, Wiley.

Helmholtz, H.L.F. von (1856-67) Treatise on Physiological Optics.

Hess, EH (1975) "The role of pupil size in communication," Scientific American, 233(5), 110–12.

Heyes, C.M. (1998) Theory of mind in nonhuman primates. Behavioral and

Brain Sciences 21, 101-48; with commentaries.

Heyes, C.M. and Galef, B.G. (eds) (1996) Social Learning in Animals: The Roots of Culture. San Diego, CA, Academic Press.

Hilgard, E.R. (1986) Divided Consciousness: Multiple Controls in Human Thought and Action. New York, Wiley.

Hocquette JF (2016) Is in vitro meat the

solution for the future? Meat Science 120:

167–176

Hodgson, R. (1891) A case of double consciousness. Proceedings of the Society for Psychical Research 7, 221-58.

Hofstadter, D.R. (1979) Code!, Escher, Bach: An Eternal Golden Braid. London, Penguin.

Hofstadter, D.R. and Dennett, D.C. (eds) (1981) The Mind's I: Fantasies and Reflections on Self and Soul. London, Penguin.

Holland, J. (ed.) (2001) Ecstasy: The Complete Guide: A Comprehensive Look at the Risks and Benefits of MDMA. Rochester, VT, Park Street Press.

Holmes, D.S. (1987) The influence of meditation versus rest on physiological arousal. In M. West (ed.) The Psychology of Meditation. Oxford, Clarendon Press, 81-103.

Holt, J. (1999) Blindsight in debates about qualia. Journal of Consciousness Studies 6(5), 54-71.

Horgan, J. (1994), 'Can science explain consciousness?', Scientific American, 271.

Holloway RL (1996) Evolution of the human brain. In: Lock A, Peters CR (eds) Handbook of human symbolic evolution. Oxford University Press, Oxford

Iacoboni M, Woods RP, Brass M, Bekkering H, Mazziotta JC, Rizzolatti G (1999) Cortical mechanisms of human imitation. Science 286: 2526–2528.

Iacoboni M, Koski LM, Brass M, Bekkering H, Woods RP, Dubeau MC, Mazziotta JC, Rizzolatti G (2001) Reafferent copies of imitated actions in the right superior temporal cortex. Proc Natl Acad Sci USA 98: 13995–13999.

Jeannerod M (1988) The neural and behavioural organization of goal-directed movements. Clarendon Press, Oxford.

Johnson-Frey SH, Maloof FR, Newman-Norlund R, Farrer C, Inati S, Grafton ST (2003) Actions or hand-objects interactions? Human inferior frontal cortex and action observation. Neuron 39: 1053–1058.

Jackson, F. (1982) Epiphenomenal qualia. Philosophical Quarterly 32, 127-36.

James, W. (1890) The Principles of Psychology (2 volumes). London, Macmillan.

James, W. (1902) The Varieties of Religious Experience: A Study in Human Nature. New York and London, Longmans, Green and Co.

Jansen, K. (2001) Ketamine: Dreams and Realities. Sarasota, FL, Multidisciplinary Association for Psychedelic Studies.

Jay, M. (ed.) (1999) Artificial Paradises: A Drugs Reader. London, Penguin.

Jaynes, J. (1976) The Origin of Consciousness in the Breakdown of the Bicameral Mind. New York, Houghton Mifflin.

Johnson, M.K. and Raye, C.L. (1981) Reality monitoring. Psychological Review 88, 67-85.

Kadim I, Mahgoub O, Baqir S et al. (2015) Cultured meat from muscle stem cells: a review of challenges and prospects. J Integr Agr 14: 222–233

Koski L, Iacoboni M, Dubeau MC, Woods RP, Mazziotta JC (2003) Modulation of cortical activity during different imitative behaviors. J Neurophysiol 89: 460–471.

Krolak-Salmon P, Henaff MA, Isnard J, Tallon-Baudry C, Guenot M, Vighetto A, Bertrand O, Mauguiere F (2003) An attention modulated response to disgust in human ventral anterior insula. Ann Neurol 53: 446–453.

Kandel, E. R. In Search of Memory: The Emergence of a New Science of Mind, W. W. Norton & Company (2007).

Kandel E. R. Schwartz JH, Jessel TM. Principles of neural sciences. New York; McGraw Hill, 2000.

Kanizsa, G. (1979), Organization In Vision (New York: Praeger).

Kaloupek DG, Scott JR, Khatami V. Assessment of coping strategies associated with syncope in blood donors. J Psychosom Res. 1985;29:207-214.

Kanwisher, N. (2001) Neural events and perceptual awareness. Cognition 79, 89-113; also reprinted inS. Dehaene (ed.) The Cognitive Neuroscience of Consciousness. Cambridge, MA, MIT Press, 89-113.

Kapleau, Roshi P. (1980) The Three Pillars of Zen: Teaching, Practice, and Enlightenment (revised edn). New York, Doubleday.

Karn, K. and Hayhoe, M. (2000) Memory representations guide

targeting eye movements in a natural task. Visual Cognition 7, 673-703.

Kasamatsu, A. and Hirai, T. (1966) An electroencephalographic study on the Zen meditation (zazen). Folia Psychiatrica et Neurologica Japonica 20, 315-36.

Kaiserman-Abramof, I. R., Graybiel, A. M., & Nauta, W. J. (1980). The thalamic projection to cortical area 17 in a congenitally anophthalmic mouse strain. Neuroscience, 5, 41–52.

Kanold, P. O., Kara, P., Reid, R. C., & Shatz, C. J. (2003). Role of subplate neurons in functional maturation of visual cortical columns. Science, 301, 521–525.

Kennedy, H., & Dehay, C. (1988). Functional implications of the anatomical organization of the callosal projections of visual areas V1 and V2 in the macaque monkey. Behav. Brain Res., 29, 225–236.

Kentridge, R.W. and Heywood, C.A. (1999) The status of blindsight. Journal of Consciousness Studies 6(5), 3-11.

Kihlstrom, J.F. (1996) Perception without awareness of what is perceived, learning without awareness of what is learned. In M. Velmans (ed.) The Science of Consciousness. London, Routledge, 23-46.

Kollerstrom, N. (1999) The path of Halley's comet, and Newton's late apprehension of the law of gravity. Annals of Science 56, 331-56.

Kosslyn, S.M. (1980) Image and Mind. Cambridge, MA, Harvard University Press.

Kosslyn, S.M. (1988) Aspects of a cognitive neuroscience of mental imagery. Science 240, 1621-6.

Kinsbourne, M. (1995), 'The intralaminar thalamic nucleii', Consciousness and Cognition, 4.

Kjaer, Troels, Camilla Bertelsen, Paola Piccini, David Brooks, Jorgen Alving, and Hans Lou. "Increased Dopamine Tone during Meditation- Induced Change of Consciousness." Cognitive Brain Research 13, no. 2 (April 2002)

Kölmel HW. 1985. Complex visual hallucinations in the hemianopic field. J Neurol Neurosurg Psychiatry.

Koenig, Harold. "Research on Religion, Spirituality, and Mental Health: A Review." Canadian Journal of Psychiatry 54, no. 5 (May 2009)

Koenig, Harold, ed. Handbook of Religion and Mental Health. San Diego, CA: Academic Press, 1998

Kraepelin E. Psychiatry: A Textbook for Students and Physicians. New York, NY: Science History Publications; 1990.

Lauglin, Charles, John McManus, and Eugene d'Aquili. Brain, Symbol, and

Experience. 2nd ed. New York: Columbia University Press, 1992

Lakoff, G. and M. Johnson (1999). Philosophy in the flesh. Basic Books: New York.

LeDoux, J. E. (1996). The emotional brain. New York: Simon & Schuster.

LeDoux, J.E. (1992), 'Emotion and the amygdala', in The Amygdala: Neurobiological Aspects of Emo- tion, Memory and Mental Dysfunction, ed J.P. Aggleton (New York: Wiley-Liss).

Levin, D.T. and Simons, D.J. (1997) Failure to detect changes to attended objects in motion pictures. Psychonomic Bulletin and Review 4, 501-6.

Levine,J. (1983) Materialism and qualia: the explanatory gap. Pacific Philosophical Quarterly 64, 354-61.

Levine,J. (2001) Purple Haze: The Puzzle of Consciousness. New York,

Oxford University Press. Levine, S. (1979) A Gradual Awakening. New York, Doubleday.

Levinson, B.W. (1965) States of awareness during general anaesthesia. British Journal of Anaesthesia 37, 544-6.

Lewicki, P., Czyzewska, M. and Hoffman, H. (1987) Unconscious acquisition of complex procedural knowledge. Journal of Experimental Psychology: Learning, Memory and Cognition 13, 523-30.

Lewicki, P., Hill, T. and Bizot, E. (1988) Acquisition of procedural knowledge about a pattern of stimuli that cannot be articulated. Cognitive Psychology 20, 24-37.

Lewicki, P., Hill, T. and Czyzewska, M. (1992) Nonconscious acquisition of information. American Psychologist 47, 796-801.

Manthey S, Schubotz RI, von Cramon DY (2003). Premotor cortex in observing erroneous action: an fMRI study. Brain Res Cogn Brain Res 15: 296–307.

Mesulam MM, Mufson EJ (1982) Insula of the old world monkey. III: Efferent cortical output and comments on function. J Comp Neurol 212: 38–52.

Naskar, Abhijit. "Homo: A Brief History of Consciousness", 2015

Naskar, Abhijit. "What is Mind?", 2016

Naskar, Abhijit. "In Search of Divinity: Journey to The Kingdom of Conscience", 2016

Naskar, Abhijit. "Love, God & Neurons: Memoir of A Scientist who found himself by getting lost", 2016

Naskar, Abhijit. "Neurons of Jesus: Mind of A Teacher, Spouse & Thinker", 2017

Naskar, Abhijit. "The Islamophobic Civilization: Voyage of Acceptance", 2017

Naskar, Abhijit. "Principia Humanitas", 2017

Naskar, Abhijit. "We Are All Black: A Treatise on Racism", 2017

Naskar, Abhijit. "Wise Mating: A Treatise on Monogamy", 2017

Naskar, Abhijit. "Illusion of Religion: A Treatise on Religious Fundamentalism", 2017

Naskar, Abhijit. "I Am The Thread: My Mission", 2017

Naskar, Abhijit. "The Bengal Tigress: A Treatise on Gender Equality", 2017

Naskar, Abhijit. "Morality Absolute", 2017

Naskar, Abhijit. "Build Bridges not Walls: In the name of Americana", 2018

Naskar, Abhijit. "Fabric of Humanity", 2018

Naskar, Abhijit. "Lives To Serve Before I Sleep", 2019

Naskar, Abhijit. "The Constitution of The United Peoples of Earth", 2019

Naskar, Abhijit. "Neurons Giveth, Neurons Taketh Away | Abhijit Naskar | TEDxIIMRanchi", 2019 https://www.youtube.com/watch?v=BNX-Q0ySm80

Naskar, Abhijit. "Mission Reality", 2019

Naskar, Abhijit. "Operation Justice: To Make A Society That Needs No Law", 2019

Naskar, Abhijit. "Every Generation Needs Caretakers: The Gospel of Patriotism", 2020

Newberg, Andrew, and Jeremy Iversen. "The Neural Basis of the Complex Mental Task of Meditation:

Neurotransmitter and Neurochemical Considerations." Medical Hypotheses 61, no. 2 (2003).

Newberg, Andrew. "How God Changes Your Brain: An Introduction to Jewish Neurotheology", CCAR Journal: The Reform Jewish Quarterly, Winter 2016.

Newberg, Andrew, and Stephanie Newberg. "A Neuropsychological Perspective on Spiritual Development." In Handbook of Spiritual Development in Childhood and Adolescence, edited by Eugene Roehlkepartain, Pamela King, Linda Wagener, and Peter Benson. London: Sage Publications, Inc., 2005

Newberg, Andrew. "The Neurotheology Link An Intersection Between Spirituality and Health", Alternative and Complimentary Therapies, Vol 21 No 1, February 2015.

Newberg, Andrew, Nancy Wintering, Dharma Khalsa, Hannah Roggenkamp, and Mark Waldman. "Meditation Effects on Cognitive Function and Cerebral Blood Flow in Subjects with Memory Loss: A Preliminary Study." Journal of Alzheimer's Disease 20, no. 2 (2010)

Nash, M. (1995), 'Glimpses of the mind', Time.

Nesse RM. Proximate and evolutionary studies of anxiety, stress and depression: synergy at the interface. Neurosci Biobehav Rev. 1999;23:895-903.

Nicolelis, Miguel. (2011) "Beyond Boundaries: The New Neuroscience of Connecting Brains with Machines--- and How It Will Change Our Lives", Times Books

O'Hara, K. and Scutt, T. (1996) There is no hard problem of consciousness. Journal of Consciousness Studies 3(4),

290-302, reprinted in J. Shear (ed.) (1997) Explaining Consciousness. Cambridge, MA, MIT Press, 69-82.

O'Regan, J.K. (1992) Solving the "real" mysteries of visual perception: the world as an outside memory. Canadian Journal of Psychology 46, 461-88.

O'Regan, J.K. and Noe, A. (2001) A sensorimotor account of vision and visual consciousness. Behavioral and Brain Sciences 24(5), 883-917.

O'Regan, J.K., Rensink, R.A. and Clark,].]. (1999) Change-blindness as a result of "mudsplashes." Nature 398, 34.

Ornstein, R.E. (1977) The Psychology of Consciousness (2nd edn). New York, Harcourt.

Ornstein, R.E. (1986) The Psychology of Consciousness (3rd edn). New York, Pehguin.

Ornstein, R.E. (1992) The Evolution of Consciousness. New York, Touchstone.

Penfield W, Faulk ME (1955) The insula: further observations on its function. Brain 78: 445– 470.

Penrose, R. (1994), Shadows of the Mind (Oxford: Oxford University Press).

Penrose, R. (1989), The Emperor's New Mind: Concerning Computers, Minds and The Laws of Physics (Oxford: Oxford University Press).

Persinger, "'I would kill in God's name' role of sex, weekly church attendance, report of a religious experience and limbic lability" Perceptual and Motor Skills 1997.

Persinger "Experimental simulation of the God experience" Neurotheology 2003.

Persinger, M. A. (1993b). Personality changes following brain injury as a grief response to the loss of sense of self: Phenomenological themes as indices of local lability and neurocognitive restructuring as psycho- therapy. Psychological Reports, 72

Persinger, Corradini, Clement, Keaney, et al "Neurotheology and its convergence with neuroquantology" NeuroQuantology 2010.

Persinger, Koren and St-Pierre "The electromagnetic induction of mystical and altered states within the laboratory" Journal of Consciousness Exploration and Research 2010.

Persinger "Case report: A prototypical spontaneous 'sensed presence' of a sentient being and concomitant electroencephalographic activity in the clinical laboratory" Neurocase 2008.

Persinger and Saroka "Potential production of Hughlings Jackson's "parasitic consciousness" by physiologically-patterned weak transcerebral magnetic fields: QEEG and source localization" Epilepsy & Behavior 28 (2013).

Persinger. "The neuropsychiatry of paranormal experiences". J Neuropsychiatry Clin Neurosci 2001.

Persinger. "Neuropsychological bases of god beliefs", New York: Praeger, 1987

Persinger. "Temporal lobe epileptic signs and correlative behaviors displayed by normal populations", Journal of General Psychology, 1986

Perry BD, Pollard R. Homeostasis, stress, trauma, and adaptation. A neurodevelopmental view of childhood trauma. Child Adolesc Psychiatr Clin N Am. 1998;7:33.

Paré, D. & Llinás, R. (1995), 'Conscious and preconscious processes as seen from the standpoint of sleep-waking cycle neurophysiology', Neuropsychologia, 33.

P. S. de Laplace. Essai Philosophique sur les Probabilites [1814], in Academy des Sciences, Oeuvres Complotes de Laplace, Vol. 7, Gauthier-Villars, Paris (1886).

Perrett DI, Harries MH, Bevan R, Thomas S, Benson PJ, Mistlin AJ, Chitty AJ, Hietanen JK, Ortega JE (1989) Frameworks of analysis for the neural representation of animate objects and actions. J Exp Bio 146: 87–113.

Phillips ML, Young AW, Senior C, Brammer M, Andrew C, Calder AJ, Bullmore ET, Perrett DI, Rowland D, Williams SC, Gray JA, David AS (1997) A specific neural substrate for perceiving facial expressions of disgust. Nature 389: 495–498.

Phillips ML, Young AW, Scott SK, Calder AJ, Andrew C, Giampietro V, Williams SC, Bullmore ET, Brammer M, Gray JA (1998) Neural responses to facial and vocal expressions of fear and disgust. Proc R Soc Lond B Biol Sci 265: 1809–1817.

Puce A, Perrett D (2003) Electrophysiological and brain imaging of biological motion. Philosoph Trans Royal Soc Lond, Series B, 358: 435–445.

Ramachandran VS. Behavioral and magnetoencephalographic correlates of plasticity in the adult human brain. Proc Natl Acad Sci USA 1993; 90: 10413–20.

Ramachandran VS. Phantom limbs, neglect syndromes, repressed memories, and Freudian psychology. Int Rev Neurobiol 1994; 37: 291–333.

Ramachandran VS. Plasticity and functional recovery in neurology. Clin Med 2005; 5: 368–73.

Ramachandran VS, Hirstein W. The perception of phantom limbs. The D. O. Hebb lecture. Brain 1998; 121: 1603–30.

Ramachandran VS, Rogers-Ramachandran D, Cobb S. Touching the phantom limb. Nature 1995; 377: 489–90.

Ramachandran VS, Rogers-Ramachandran D. Phantom limbs and neural plasticity. Arch Neurol 2000; 57: 317–20.

Ramachandran VS, Rogers-Ramachandran D. It's all done with mirrors. Sci Am Mind 2007; 18: 16–9.

Ramachandran VS, Rogers-Ramachandran D. Sensations referred to a patient's phantom arm from another subjects intact arm: perceptual correlates of mirror neurons. Med Hypotheses 2008; 70: 1233–4.

Ramachandran VS, Rogers-Ramachandran D, Stewart M. Perceptual correlates of massive cortical reorganization. Science 1992; 258: 1159–60.

Rizzolatti G, Craighero L (2004) The mirror-neuron system. Annu Rev Neurosci 27: 169–192.

Rizzolatti G, Fogassi L, Gallese V (2001) Neurophysiological mechanisms underlying the understanding and imitation of action. Nature Rev Neurosci 2:661–670.

Rock I, Victor J. Vision and touch: an experimentally created conflict between the two senses. Science 1964; 143: 594–6.

Rose´n B, Lundborg G. Training with a mirror in rehabilitation of the hand. Scand J Plast Reconstr Surg Hand Surg 2005; 39: 104–8.

Royet JP, Plailly J, Delon-Martin C, Kareken DA, Segebarth C (2003) fMRI of emotional responses to odors: influence of hedonic valence and judgment, handedness, and gender. Neuroimage 20: 713–728.

Rozin R Haidt J and McCauley CR (2000) Disgust. In: Lewis M, Haviland-Jones JM (eds) Handbook of Emotion. 2nd Edition. Guilford Press, New York, pp 637–653.

Saxe R, Carey S, Kanwisher N (2004) Understanding other minds: linking developmental psychology and functional neuroimaging. Annu Rev Psychol 55: 87–124.

S. J. Russell and P. Norvig, Artificial intelligence: a modern approach (3rd edition): Prentice Hall, 2009.

Schienle A, Stark R, Walter B, Blecker C, Ott U, Kirsch P, Sammer G, Vaitl D (2002) The insula is not specifically involved in disgust processing: an fMRI study. Neuroreport 13: 2023–2026.

Showers MJC, Lauer EW (1961) Somatovisceral motor patterns in the insula. J Comp Neurol 117: 107–115.

Singer T, Seymour B, O'Doherty J, Kaube H, Dolan RJ, Frith CD (2004) Empathy for pain involves the affective but not the sensory components of pain. Science 303: 1157–1162.

Smith A (1759) The theory of moral sentiments (ed. 1976). Clarendon Press, Oxford.

S. N. Bose (1924). "Plancks Gesetz und Lichtquantenhypothese". Zeitschrift für Physik. 26 (1): 178–181.

Sprengelmeyer R, Rausch M, Eysel UT, Przuntek H (1998) Neural structures associated with recognition of facial expressions of basic emotions Proc R Soc Lond B Biol Sci 265: 1927–1931.

Strafella AP, Paus T (2000) Modulation of cortical excitability during action observation: a transcranial magnetic stimulation study. NeuroReport 11: 2289–2292.

Simonsen R (2015) Eating for the future: veganism and the challenge of in vitro meat. In: Stapleton P, Byers A (Hg). Biopolitics and utopia. Palgrave Macmillan, New York (2015), S 167–190

Tanaka K (1996) Inferotemporal cortex and object vision. Ann Rev Neurosci. 19: 109–140.

Tesla N. "My Inventions", 1919

T. R. Society, "Machine learning: the power and promise of computers that learn by example," ed. The Royal Society, 2017.

Tomasello M, Call J (1997) Primate cognition. Oxford University Press, Oxford.

Tremblay C, Robert M, Pascual-Leone A, Lepore F, Nguyen DK, Carmant L, Bouthillier A, Theoret H (2004) Action observation and execution: intracranial recordings in a human subject. Neurology. 63: 937–938.

Umilta MA, Kohler E, Gallese V, Fogassi L, Fadiga L, Keysers C, Rizzolatti G (2001) "I know what you are doing": a neurophysiological study. Neuron 32: 91–101.

Von Wright G.H., (1963), Norm and Action. A Logical Inquiry, Routledge & Kegan Paul, London.

Von Wright G.H., (1976), "Determinism and the Study of Man", in Essays on Explanation and Understanding, ed. by J. Manninen and R. Tuomela, Reidel, Dordrecht.

Von Wright G.H., (1977), "What is Humanism?", The Lindlay Lecture, University of Arkansas, Lawrence, Kansas.

Von Wright G.H., (1979), "Humanism and the Humanities", in Philosophy and Grammar, ed. by S. Kanger and S. Öhman, Reidel, Dordrecht, pp. 1-16. Reprinted in von Wright (1993).

Von Wright G.H., (1980), Freedom and Determination, North-Holland Publishing Co., Amsterdam.

Von Wright G.H., (1985), Of Human Freedom, The Tanner Lectures on Human Values,

Vol. VI, ed. by S. M. McMurrin, University of Utah Press, Salt Lake City, pp. 107-70. Reprinted in von Wright (1998).

Von Wright G.H., (1993), The Tree of Knowledge and Other Essays, Brill, Leiden.

Von Wright G.H., (1997), "Progress: Fact and Fiction", in The Idea of Progress, ed. by A. Burgen et al., W. de Gruyter, Berlin, pp. 1-18.

Von Wright G.H., (1998), In the Shadow of Descartes: Essays in the Philosophy of Mind, Kluwer, Dordrecht.

MAD ABOUT HUMANS